Raptor on a tractor

Russell Punter

Illustrated by David Semple

Farmer Raptor's working hard.
He's in the fields today.

His tractor drags a rake along.
Then he makes bales of hay.

By noon, his tummy's rumbling.

His farmhouse lies five miles away.
He chugs off down a track.

The bridge ahead is broken.

He has the whole road to himself.
That isn't going to last...

Triceratops slows to a stop.

Speed up.
I can't get past!

"I'm heading to the County Fair.
You're going to make me late!"

"Don't panic, guys! I have a plan.
I'll free you all," says Raptor.

He fixes ropes between each car,
then ties one to his tractor.

He hauls them out in one long row,
and pulls them down the road.

When Raptor's "tractor train" arrives,
the folk all stand and stare.

Then everybody wants a turn...
It's the BEST ride at the Fair!

Starting to read

Even before children start to recognize words, they can learn about the pleasures of reading. Encouraging a love of stories and a joy in language is the best place to start.

About phonics

When children learn to read in school, they are often taught to recognize words through phonics. This teaches them to identify the sounds of letters that are then put together to make words. An important first step is for children to hear rhymes, which help them to listen out for the sounds in words.

You can find out more about phonics on the Usborne website at **usborne.com/Phonics**

Phonics Readers

These rhyming books provide the perfect combination of fun and phonics. They are lively and entertaining with great storylines and quirky illustrations. They have the added bonus of focusing on certain sounds so in this story your child will soon identify the *a* sound, as in **Raptor** and **tractor.** Look out, too, for rhymes such as **snack – track** and **road – towed.**

Reading with your child

If your child is reading a story to you, don't rush to correct mistakes, but be ready to prompt or guide if needed. Above all, give plenty of praise and encouragement.

Edited by Lesley Sims
Designed by Hope Reynolds

Reading consultants: Alison Kelly and Anne Washtell

First published in 2024 by Usborne Publishing Limited, 83-85 Saffron Hill, London EC1N 8RT, United Kingdom. usborne.com Copyright © 2024 Usborne Publishing Limited. The name Usborne and the Balloon logo are registered trade marks of Usborne Publishing Limited.